The Ultimate Sleepover Party Book

There are tons of delicious recipes and fun crafts in this book, many of which require the use of an oven, microwave, stove, sharp utensils, and objects. Please make sure to have a grown-up on hand to assist you or to supervise.

The Ultimate Sleepover Party Book

Debra Mostow Zakarin

Illustrated by Sarah Gibb

SCHOLASTIC INC.

New York Toronto London Auckland Sydney
Mexico City New Delhi Hong Kong

For Gina – my sister-in-law,
dear friend, and ultimate lunch buddy.

ISBN 0-439-21182-4

Published by Scholastic Inc.,
555 Broadway, New York, NY 10012,
by arrangement with Element Books, Inc.

12 11 10 9 8 7 6 5 4 3 2 0 1 2 3 4 5/0

Printed in the U.S.A. 40

First Scholastic printing, September 2000

Cover design by Mandy Sherliker
Cover illustration by Sue Clarke
Typeset by Dorchester Typesetting Group Ltd.

Contents

Hello from the Author 7
Are you ready to throw the ultimate sleepover party? 8
Inside and Outside Makeover Party 14
Friendship Quiz 25
Carnival Party 32
Happening Hollywood Party 41
Super Sleuth Party 51
Quiz: Do you act your age? 60
Cool Crafts Party 67
Astrology Party 74
Valentine's Day Party 86
Valentine Quiz: Is he the boy for you? 90
Picnic Party 96
Talent Show Party 102
Beauty Quiz 108
New Year's Eve Party 111
Party Dos and Don'ts 115
Party memories 119
My sleepover party 121
My sleepover sign-in 123

ACKNOWLEDGEMENTS

Thanks to Barry Cunningham and Mike Powell at Element Children's Books. Thanks to all the wonderful girls who shared their stories with me and to all my friends whose sleepover party memories brought me back to a very happy place. And finally, thanks to my husband Scott and son Caleb – my best friends.

HELLO FROM THE AUTHOR

I loved parties – especially sleepover parties! I was in the sixth grade when I hosted my first sleepover party. And, let me tell you, it was pretty ultimate.

What was the theme? Ice cream (chocolate is my all time favorite flavor)! I made invitations in the shape of ice-cream cones and invited the girls in my class – all **15** of them came!

Everyone brought sleeping bags and pillows and we slept in one big circle in the family room. We made our own sundaes, watched *Willy Wonka and the Chocolate Factory*, played *Twister*, made up new dances, talked about boys (a lot!), and told ghost stories. I stayed up the whole night and, girl, was I exhausted the next day – I went straight to sleep after all my friends left.

We cooked waffles in the morning and topped them with, what else, ice cream! As everyone was leaving they signed their names on a white pillowcase and I handed out flavored lip-gloss as the party favor. And, guess what flavor it was? Chocolate! Since I was such a chocolate freak my friends thought it was the bomb of a party favor!

To this day, I still love looking at the photo album filled with memories from my very first sleepover party.

I hope that after reading this book you'll throw some ultimate sleepover parties and create *your* very own memories to have forever!

Debra Mostow Zakarin

ARE YOU READY TO THROW THE ULTIMATE SLEEPOVER PARTY?

Anybody can throw an ordinary dull sleepover party, but what about if you want to have the *ultimate* sleepover party? The party that your friends and you will be talking about for days on end afterward. Do you know what to do? Where to begin? Have no fear: *The Ultimate Sleepover Party Book* will guide you through all stages of party planning.

When you go to a sleepover party just have a great time, stay up all night, laugh a lot and eat.

Sari F.

Ultimate Sleepover Checklist

First things first

- Get parents' OK to host a sleepover party. (Um, this is a biggie!)
- How many friends do you want to invite?
- Where will you all sleep?
- Okay, now figure out if you have enough room for all the people that you'd like to invite. Not enough room? Start cutting the list. And remember small sleepover parties are just as much fun as large ones.
- Figure out how much money you can spend.
- Decide on a theme. (This will depend somewhat on how much you can spend – some parties will cost more than others.)
- Pick a date.

Four weeks before party

- Make invitations. Email, send or hand them out.
- Create a list of everything you'll need to make this the ultimate sleepover party.

Two weeks before party

- Create or buy party treats and decorations.
- Plan menu.
- Plan games.
- Get the music ready.

One week before party

- Shop till you drop for food, paper goods, and how about a new pair of PJs?

Two days before party

- Bake, bake, bake.
- Cook, cook, cook.

One day before party

- Clean your house.
- Set up decorations.
- Wrap up party treats.

Day of party

- Take a NAP!!!

Party Etiquette

Be sensitive

If inviting all the girls in your class then

you can feel comfortable handing out invitations. However, if only inviting a handful of girls from your class, make sure to mail or email invitations to your friends' homes so as not to hurt anybody's feelings and rub it in her face that she was not invited.

In the know

Invitations don't have to be expensive, but they do set the mood of the party. Make sure to include all important information on the invitation such as:

- Party theme
- Date
- Arrival time and departure time for the next morning
- Address and telephone number
- Special instructions like whether your guests need to bring a sleeping bag, dress a certain way, or bring certain items to your house.

BYOSB (bring your own sleeping bag)

Ice breakers

If not everyone knows each other then try this as an ice-breaker once all your guests arrive and before the party really gets going. Sit around in a circle; introduce yourselves, say where you live and how you know the hostess of the party. For some extra added giggles play a round of "pass the orange." Everybody stands in a circle and you pass an orange to the person on your right. Sound easy? Not really. You can't use your hands – just your neck.

To open or not to open

One of the best things about a party is the presents – there, I said it. But, think twice before opening up your gifts in front of all your guests. Not everybody may have bought or made you something and you wouldn't want that person to feel badly.

The Morning After

Eyes puffy from too little sleep? Pass out chilled slices of cucumber and gently place them over your eyelids. Set out a basket filled to the brim with hair bands, rubber bands, and scrunchies. This way, nobody will feel embarrassed about morning hair at the breakfast table.

Don't have enough money to buy party treats? Well, now's the time to put your creative talents to good use – make them!

Cool Party Treats (you can make or buy)

Bookmarks, compact mirror, lip gloss, bouquet of balloons, snapshots, candy, hair barrettes, nail polish, markers, rubber stamps, magnets, keychains, pins, earrings, photo albums, autograph books, picture frames, friendship award certificates, mouse pad, pencils wrapped in ribbon, yo-yos, small stuffed animals, playing cards, and beaded ankle bracelets.

It's not Over Yet

Try to send out thank-you notes the first week after your party is over. Thank your friends for any gifts they may have given you and for the special memories. Don't have any thank-you notes? How about making a postcard out of a photo from your party? Mail them, hand them out, or stick them in your friend's lunch bag when she isn't looking.

INSIDE AND OUTSIDE MAKEOVER PARTY

Take the time with your friends this evening to feel good about yourselves both inside and out. Without doing anything *too* drastic (like having your best friend cut your hair or sneaking out in the middle of the night to a 24-hour tattoo parlor), experiment with changing your look. If you usually wear your hair down how about putting it up in clips? Or why not get out of your jeans and T-shirt and try on a knee-length skirt with a cropped T?

I love slumber parties. I love calling boys. I love checking out the fun pajamas, eating, seeing who could stay awake the latest, and who falls asleep first.

Wendy B.

Setting the Stage

There are many cool invitations you can make for a makeover party. Using an 8-inch by 11-inch piece of paper, glue some fake nails around the edge to create a fun border.

Or make a mirror invitation. Here's what you'll need: thick construction paper or thick card stock paper

- aluminum foil
- glue
- tape
- scissors
- markers

With your pencil cut out any shape of mirror that you choose. It could be round, square, or even rectangular. Don't make it too small – you'll need enough room to write the invitations. Next, on one side of the thick paper glue on the tin foil – this is the "mirror" side. On the other side, using different colored markers, write out the invitation.

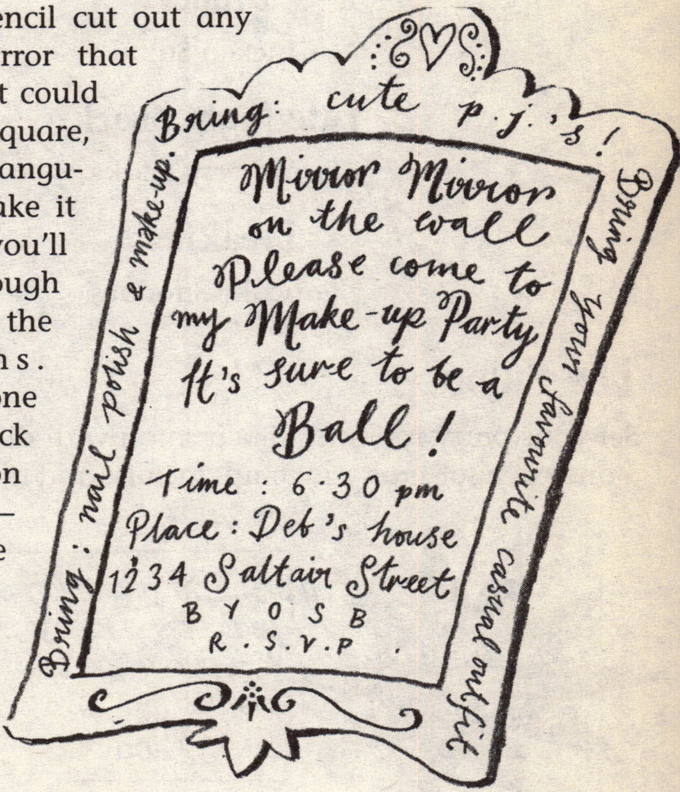

Makeover Menu

Munchies

Veggies and Dip
Baked (not fried) potato chips
Assorted Nuts

Dinner

Chicken Salad

Late Night Snack

Strawberry Shake

Breakfast

Pancake Sundaes

The Salon

Set your party room up like a salon with different stations – one each for hair, make-up, facials, and nails.

Take before and after photos

It's fun to give each other manicure and pedicures and try on your friend's clothes.

Cindy C.

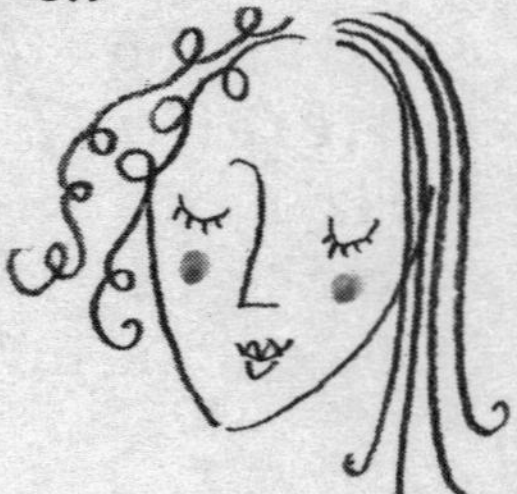

Hair

Set out hair accessories such as brushes, combs, barrettes, scrunchies, ribbons, clips, blow-dryers, straightening iron, curling iron, and gels. Take turns washing each other's hair in the bathroom or kitchen sink. Now, start styling. Straighten curly hair, curl straight hair, slick back short hair, and put long hair up in a braid.

Facial

Gently wash your face with a moisturizing soap and rinse with warm water followed by cold. (This will close your pores up.) For some extra face-cleansing mix 1 cup oatmeal with 1 cup honey and 1 table-spoon almonds finely ground. (Use a food processor or blender.) Spread this mixture over your face (avoiding the eye area) and throat (the much neglected part of the face) and let it set for about 10 minutes. Rinse off with cool water.

One of the girls from my class had a sleepover party. I went to the party, but I didn't have any fun. When I got there I could tell that the girls had been saying mean things about me behind my back. Sometimes they do stuff like that. Nobody wanted to be my partner for any of the games and I always got stuck sitting at a seat at the end of the table. I tried to act like I didn't notice that anyone was talking behind my back, but it was really hard to do. I couldn't eat because I had a lump in my throat from fighting back tears. I felt lonely all night long trying to stay awake in my sleeping bag — I was afraid that if I fell asleep someone would play nasty tricks on me. I couldn't wait for the party to be over. I couldn't stop crying when I got into my mom's car the next morning. She pulled over to the side of the road and just held me. I made her promise not to call any of the girls' mothers — I knew it would just make things worse. Sometimes girls can be so mean!

Marie B.

Make-Up

Don't forget to wash off your make-up before going to sleep — you don't want to wake up with a big zit!

Arrange yours and your friends' make-up in front of a well-lit mirror. Apply your own or take turns making each other over. Set out plenty of cotton balls, cotton swabs, and tissues so that you don't have to share make-up applicators. (This will keep everything sanitary.)

Have some fashion magazines on hand and use an ad of a model you like as your make-up inspiration and guide.

Nails

Have tons of different color nail polish available, as well as fake nails and nail decals. Try painting each nail a different color. Oh, and don't forget the toes – pedicures are perfectly pampering.

Once you're all done doing your hair, make-up and nails put on your favorite casual outfits and have a makeover fashion show. Vote on the most original hairstyle, best make-up job, wackiest nails, and cutest toes. Give out compact mirrors to the winners.

One time someone put toothpaste in my hands when I fell asleep and then tickled my face. When I went to scratch my face I got minty goo all over it.

Jennifer R.

Recipe Corner

Pancake Sundaes

For 8 – 12 pancakes, you'll need:

1 egg
1 cup all-purpose flour, sifted
1 cup milk
1 tablespoon sugar
2 tablespoons vegetable oil
3 teaspoons baking powder
1 teaspoon salt

Beat the egg until fluffy. Add the rest of the ingredients and mix until smooth. Grease a hot skillet and drop a serving spoonful onto the skillet with one spoonful for each pancake. When each spoonful bubbles and the edges are brown, turn over to cook the other side.

Now, let's add the toppings to make it a "sundae."

3 bananas, split in half and quartered
1 large carton strawberry yogurt
1 large carton vanilla yogurt

Top each pancake with two banana pieces and one scoop

each of the strawberry and vanilla yogurts.

Who wouldn't want to wake up to this breakfast?!

Chicken Salad

This delicious chicken salad can be made the night before your party. Take the time to prepare it before your guests arrive. This way, you won't be slaving in the kitchen while your friends are in the other room having fun!

Makes about 4 servings:

½ cup vinaigrette dressing

1 teaspoon Dijon mustard

1 pound cooked chicken (meat from a barbecued or roasted deli chicken) cut into large chunks

Slivers of red or yellow bell pepper (2 peppers)

Fresh romaine lettuce or spinach, washed

Combine vinaigrette with the mustard; season to taste with salt and pepper and toss with the chicken. Next, toss the chicken with the bell peppers and serve over washed lettuce; serve some extra dressing on the side.

Cucumber and Yogurt Dip

Makes about 1½ cups

1 medium cucumber, peeled, seeded, and chopped (hint: the easiest way to seed a cucumber is by first slicing it in half lengthwise and then scooping the seeds out with a spoon)

1 cup plain low-fat yogurt

1 garlic clove crushed through a press

2 tablespoons fresh dill

Salt and pepper

In a medium bowl, stir together the cucumber, yogurt, garlic and dill. Season lightly with salt and pepper. Cover tightly and refrigerate until ready to serve.

Baked Potato Chips

Depending upon how much time you have either buy a few bags of baked potato chips or try making a batch yourself!

Makes about 70 chips

2 large baking potatoes

Salt

Paprika

Preheat oven to 300°F. First scrub the potatoes very well. Next, with the skin on (that's where most of the nutrients are) slice the potatoes very thinly. A food processor will make this process much easier and you won't run the risk of cutting yourself. Okay, after the potatoes have been sliced, spread them in a single layer on a large wire rack which is set over a baking pan. Season with salt and paprika. Place them in the oven and bake for 50 minutes, or until potatoes are crisp and lightly browned. Let the potatoes cool and store them in a bag until ready to serve. Oh, and try not to eat them all before your guests arrive. Bet you can't!

Strawberry Shake

Makes two shakes

1 cup skim milk

1 cup strawberries (without the stems)

1 teaspoon vanilla extract

1 teaspoon sugar (optional)

1 cup ice cubes

Place milk, strawberries, vanilla extract, sugar, and ice cubes in a blender (or even a food processor). Blend about 30 seconds, until smooth.

Don't like strawberries? Well, substitute blueberries, raspberries or blackberries. Or, for a really fancy shake, blend together an assortment of berries.

When I was planning my sleepover party I had this really tough problem. I had two best friends. One friend was from school, Cherise, and one friend was from camp, Devra. They were both really different from each other. And, did I mention that Cherise and Devra just hated each other? Well, they did. I knew I was going to invite them both even though it was making me feel kind of nervous. Anyway, when I gave Cherise her invitation she asked me if I was inviting Devra. I said yes. She then asked me if I had sent Devra her invitation (Devra doesn't live in our town). I shook my head no. Then, Cherise did something that totally shocked me! She handed me back my invitation and said, "if you invite Devra then don't bother inviting me." I just stood there with my mouth open. I didn't know what to say — which is very unusual for me! "It's not too hard to understand," she continued. "If you give me back the invitation tomorrow I'll know that you decided to not to invite Devra and then I'll be more than happy to go to your sleep-over party." I felt really mad at Cherise and also kind of scared of her. Would she not be my friend if I invited her and Devra? Would she really not come? Would she turn everyone against me? I could barely concentrate that day in school. At the end of the day she said goodbye and smiled as if nothing was wrong. I felt sick to my stomach. That night, I told my older brother (he's six-teen and really smart) what Cherise said to me during recess and asked him what he would do if he were me. He told me that Cherise wasn't a true friend because she was making me choose between her and Devra. He said, if he was me he would just hand Cherise the invitation and say, "I'm inviting Devra and you and I hope you both can come." I knew he was right and took his advice. I was so nervous when I gave Cherise her invitation and said what my brother had told me to say. Anyway, Cherise never came to my party. And, you know what's weird? I had a really good time without her. I realized just how bossy she used to be and how much more comfortable I am when she is not around. And all my other friends from school really liked Devra! Yeah!

Annie A.

Party treats

Fill a bag with rubber bands, small soaps, and a nail file.

FRIENDSHIP QUIZ

Is your best friend really the best?

So, is your best friend really the best? If you and your gal pals are ready to put your friendship to the test than this quiz is for you. Take the quiz separately and compare results at the end. Be as honest as possible. Now would be a great time for all of you to have an open conversation about friendship and what it means to each of you.

1. **Day after day you've been dragging your best friend to the mall because you have the ultimate crush on the guy who works at the pizza place. After two weeks of this, she**

a. is sick of all your childish crushes – she's not going!

b. jokingly says she is getting tired of Italian food, but will go with you anyway;

c. reminds you of the last guy you liked who worked at the pizza place – the one with melted cheese for brains (oops, almost forgot about him).

2. There's only one seat available at the lunch table where the most popular girls sit. While you and your best friend are walking past the table, the most popular girl turns to your best friend and asks her to join the group. Your best friend

a. is sitting down at the table before she can even yell, "see you in math class;"

b. kindly declines and explains that there isn't room for two;

c. sits down and offers you the corner of her chair.

3. You just started dating your cousin's best friend. You

a. keep it a secret from your best friend because she's a total flirt with every guy you like;

b. can't wait for them to meet – maybe he has a friend for her;

c. hold off telling her because even though she'll act happy for you – sometimes you're just not sure about how sincere she really is.

4. **The smartest girl in class passes a note to your best friend accusing you of cheating. Your friend**
   a. looks at you as if you'd just robbed a bank;
   b. rips it up immediately;
   c. doesn't believe it, but passes the note to the girl next to her.

5. **You and your best friend both try out for parts in the school play. You find out that your friend got the lead role and you're just an extra. Your friend**
   a. starts screaming, "I'm going to be a star!"
   b. says that the director must be out of his mind and in her book you're an award-winning friend;
   c. suggests that maybe you could be her understudy.

6. **Your parakeet, Pickles, just died and you call your friend in tears. She**
   a. makes a joke that she'll be sending her cat Fluffy right over for an afternoon snack;

b. is over to your house looking at pictures of Pickles with you before you even have a chance to hang up the phone;

c. Offers her condolences and asks to borrow your history notes.

7. You and your friend have plans to go to the movies on Saturday afternoon. On Friday night the cutest boy in your class invites her to go roller-blading with him – on Saturday afternoon! Your friend

a. asks to borrow your skates, then tells you why she needs them;

b. sweetly declines the cutest boy's invitation and suggests they go on Sunday afternoon;

c. would never think of ditching you for a boy – so she brings him along to the movies.

8. Uh-oh! As you're getting ready for your grandmother's 85th birthday party you realize you didn't get her a card. In a panic you call your best friend. She

a. tells you not to worry about it – since your grandmother's blind she'll never even notice;

b. quickly designs a beautiful card right on her computer and runs it over to your house;

c. sympathetically says, "oh, no!" and asks if she could call you back – she's right in the middle of a movie.

9. **When it comes right down to it, you know that you can tell your best friend**
   a. pretty much nothing – she's worse than all the tabloids put together;
   b. absolutely everything – she'd take any secret to the grave;
   c. almost anything – you just have to be careful. Your friend's heart is in the right place, but unfortunately she babbles on a bit too much to others.

10. **Your gang of girlfriends is seeing 98° in concert. You were supposed to be there too, but are sick at home with the flu. Your best-friend**
   a. takes two days to call you after the concert – she's on cloud 98;
   b. buys you a T-shirt and tells you it would have been even more fun if you were there;
   c. calls you immediately, tells you all about the concert, but forgets to ask how you're feeling.

11. **It's Sunday night and you're freaking out because you've blown off your Social Studies paper until the very last minute. You call your best friend, she**

a. asks you to speak up – she's printing out her 25-page paper and can't hear you over her father's ancient printer;
b. admits to you that she's getting sick of what a slack you are, but agrees to help;
c. says she'll keep her fingers crossed for you that you'll be able to pull an all nighter.

12. You can always depend on your friend to

a. tell people about your most embarrassing moments;
b. make you laugh at just about anything;
c. save a seat for you on the school bus.

13. You have no doubt that when you and your friend are all grown up

a. you'll be parting ways;
b. be bridesmaids at each other's wedding;
c. make an effort to give each other a call at least twice a year.

For each question you answered with the letter **(a)** give your friend **1** point.

For each question you answered with the letter **(b)** give your friend **3** points.

For each question you answered with the letter **(c)** give your friend **2** points.

Better than best (33 to 39 points)
Your best friend is truly a gem. She really cares about you and your friendship and isn't afraid to be honest with you. This one is a keeper!

Flaky Friend (26 to 32 points)
Your best friend means well and does care about you, but she's a bit self-absorbed. Sounds as if she's worth the effort, but you need to have a heart to heart talk with her and let her know when and how she let's you down. If she's really your friend, you'll be able to work it out – together.

What are you thinking? (13 to 25 points)
With friends like this who needs enemies? This person is not a friend to you and doesn't sound as if she knows how to be a friend to anyone else. Run as fast as you can from this one and don't look back!

CARNIVAL PARTY

I try to dip the hand, of the first person that falls asleep, in warm water to see if she will pee in her sleep. Once, I even drew on someone's face when she fell asleep. But, she didn't find it so funny.

Julia B.

Step right up, step right up, and come join the carnival sleepover fun! This kind of party will take some planning because you will be setting up different game areas which will need to be done before your guests arrive.

Set up a large tent in your backyard and have the party out back. No tent? No backyard? No big deal. Set the stage in your party room. Decorate it with lots of streamers, balloons, and party hats.

Party invitations

What do you think of when you hear the word carnival? Balloons, peanuts and clowns are just some that come to mind. Following are three different invitation ideas for you to choose from.

Blow-up party invitation

1 balloon per person
Dark-colored markers with a thick point
Handful of confetti
Colorful ribbon

Before blowing up the balloon, carefully drop a handful of confetti into the mouth of the balloon. Once that's done, blow up the balloon and tie the end of it in a knot so no air can escape. With your markers, gently (if you press too hard your invitation could *pop* before your

Instant confetti: just get lots of pieces of different colored paper and cut them into very very small pieces own eyes) write out your invitation. A very light-colored balloon will work best. Not only will you be able to see the confetti that's inside, but also the markers will show up better. Lastly, tie some colorful ribbons to the end of the balloon. Hand deliver the balloon invitation to each of your guests. Mailing them is not recommended!

Peanut bag invitations

One small brown paper bag per invitation

Markers

Crayons

Tape

Lots of peanuts (the kind that's in its shell)

With your markers, write out the invitation on one side of the brown bag. Next, decorate each bag keeping in mind the carnival theme. Now fill each bag with peanuts and tape the top of the bag closed. This fun and yummy invitation should not be mailed.

Clowning Around

1 piece 8-inch by 11-inch paper per invitation

Envelopes (one per invitation)

Crayons

Markers

Draw the outline of a clown face wearing a hat on a piece of paper. Write out the invitation in the face. Go wild, be creative and have some fun with this inexpensive invitation that can be mailed to your guests.

Bring cute jammies, a clean set of clothes, and a comfortable pillow from home.

Jessica F.

Carnival Cuisine

Munchies

Peanuts
Popcorn
Potato chips

Dinner

Hot dogs and buns (serve lots of catsup, mustard, relish, and sauerkraut on the side)
Corn on the Cob
Sparkling Lemonade

Late Night Snack

Monkey Pops

Breakfast

Assorted cereals

Carnival Stations

Face painting

Buy some face paints or use lipstick, eyeliners, and make-up as your paints. Draw hearts, stars, peace signs, and clown faces.

Jelly bean jumble

Before your guests arrive fill a glass bowl with jelly beans – count them as you put them in the bowl and write that number down on a piece of paper and hide it in a safe place so you don't forget how many jelly beans you put in the bowl. Place an empty bowl and some pieces of paper and pens next to the bowl filled with the jellybeans. Have your guests write down their names and how many jelly-beans they think are in the bowl. The one who guesses the exact number or comes closest gets the bowl and jelly beans as a prize.

Pot toss

Set up six large pots one behind the other in a straight line. Place different small toys or wrapped candies into each of the pots. Establish a starting line. Each player stands behind the line and attempts to toss a small bean-bag into each of the pots. For every pot that the beanbag successfully goes into the player takes a prize from that pot. If the player misses, it's the next person's turn.

Peanut race

It's best to run this race on a carpet. Each player is given a peanut in the shell and they line up behind the start line on hands and knees. Designate the finish line about ten feet away from the start. The first player to push the peanut to the finish line with his or her nose wins!

What . . . ?

Do you think you know your friends? How well do you really know them? Sit around in a circle with your friends and ask each other these questions. You may be surprised by the answers.

What one thing really, really gets on your nerves?

What do you think it would be like to switch places with your mom for a day? What about switching places with your best friend?

What do you enjoy doing now that you don't think you'll enjoy doing in five years?

What boy in your class do you absolutely hate? What is the best thing about him?

What one thing would you change about yourself?

What one thing would you never change about yourself?

Recipe Corner

Corn on the Cob

1 ear of corn per person

Butter

Salt and pepper

Husk the corn. Wrap each ear tightly in aluminum foil. Grill on the barbecue for about 10 minutes, turning it frequently. Or, boil the corn (without the aluminum foil) for 15 minutes or until soft. Serve with butter, salt and pepper.

Sparkling Lemonade

Serves 4

3 lemons

4 tablespoons sugar (taste to see if more sugar is needed)

1 quart club soda or seltzer

Squeeze lemons and pour the juice along with one of the rinds into a pitcher with ice cubes. Add the sugar and stir well. Add the soda and serve over ice.

Monkey Pops

Makes 4 servings

This recipe should be made the morning of your party so that the pops will be frozen by the time late night munchies hit.

4 bananas

Aluminum foil

Toppings:

1) 1 tablespoon brown sugar and 1 teaspoon nutmeg (combine together)

2) 1 tablespoon honey and 1 tablespoon granola (combine together)

3) 1 tablespoon honey and 1 tablespoon crushed peanuts (combine together)

Peel and roll each banana in one of the toppings. Wrap each banana in aluminum foil and freeze. When you're ready to eat the pops just peel off the foil.

Party treats

Decorate brown bags with clown faces. Fill the bag with chocolate candies, bottle of bubbles, and stickers.

HAPPENING HOLLYWOOD PARTY

You and Me Books, girl talk and eating . . . does life get any better than that?

Jenna F.

Superstars in Hollywood don't cut any corners when it comes to celebrating – especially the night of the Oscars! Their outfits are made by some of the most famous designers in the world and they eat only the finest food. So, on the evening of your Happening

Hollywood Sleepover Party you will be serving your guests food that's good enough for a superstar!

Place a large star to the entrance of your home or party room that says: **V.I.F. (very important friends) Party Room.** Set out an autograph book and have your guests sign in as they arrive. You never know, one of their signatures may be worth something one day.

Charades

Act out the title to your favorite movie. The person who guesses the right answer gets a prize.

At my sleepover party I was scared that someone might not be nice to me.

Lindsay R.

Roll out the red carpet

Stars always walk along the red carpet. Set down a red towel or sheet and have your friends strut down the "carpet" in their cutest pajamas. Don't forget to take pictures!

Make your own movie

A couple of weeks before your party write a short movie or funny scene. Make copies of your script and hand them out to your friends. Now, grab your video camera and start directing. Once you're finished watch your movie. Give an award to the best actress.

Movies to rent

Spiceworld
Phantom Menace
The Parent Trap
Matilda
Home Alone
Titanic
Toy Story
Runaway Bride

Don't forget to return the movies in time — you don't want to be charged a late fee

Award Winning Edibles

Hors d'oeuvres

Eggplant Caviar and Crackers
Assorted Candies (your favorites will be just fine)

Dinner

Star-studded Finger Sandwiches (tuna salad, cucumber, and cream cheese and turkey)
Green Salad

Munchies

Popcorn
Breathtaking Brownies

Breakfast

Sausage Cheese Muffins
Herbal tea

Recipe Corner

Eggplant Caviar

Makes about 2 cups of Caviar

1 medium eggplant
1 tablespoon lemon juice
1 large tomato, peeled and chopped
1 medium onion, chopped
1 garlic clove, minced
2 tablespoons chopped parsley
2 tablespoons olive oil
1 teaspoon salt
1 teaspoon pepper

Preheat oven to 400°F. With a fork, pierce the eggplant in three different places. Place the eggplant in a baking dish and bake for 30 to 40 minutes, until very soft. Once the eggplant has completely cooled off, peel off the skin. Place the peeled eggplant in a medium bowl and mash it to a puree. Add the lemon juice, tomato, onion, garlic, parsley, oil, salt, and pepper. Mix very well. Cover and refrigerate until ready to serve. This eggplant caviar tastes just great on crackers.

Star-studded Finger Sandwiches

For each sandwich you will need two slices of bread. White or whole wheat work best.

Remove the crust and begin making the sandwich. Try some tuna salad or sliced turkey breast with a touch of mayonnaise and mustard, or thinly sliced cucumber with some cream cheese. Once all the sandwiches are made (figure about two sandwiches per guest) cut them into stars with a metal cookie cutter. (Plastic ones won't be able to slice through the bread as easily as a metal one.)

You'll never believe what happened at my sleepover party! After we all got washed up and changed into our paja-mas I asked everyone to sit in a circle. I shut the lights,

turned on my flashlight, and held it right under my chin. This gave my face a spooky kind of glow. Anyway, I told everyone about the lady who lived in our old house a long, long time ago. She was a nice old lady when she was alive, but since she's been dead she's been very angry because the night she died her false teeth weren't in her mouth — they were in a jar of water in the kitchen. This poor old lady was living in heaven without any teeth because nobody bothered to stick them back into her mouth when they buried her. Well, right at that moment my brother, who was listening at the door, set down on the floor wind up teeth we have. Everybody screamed and jumped into each other's arms as these teeth came chattering across the room. My brother and I, who I had planned this with before my party, couldn't stop laughing. I was laughing so hard I almost wet my pants.

Miriam M.

Breathtaking Brownies

Makes about 12 brownies

1 cup all-purpose flour, sifted
1 cup unsweetened baking cocoa
1 teaspoon salt
1 bag semi-sweet chocolate chips
3 large eggs
1 cup granulated sugar
6 tablespoons applesauce

2 tablespoons vegetable oil

1 teaspoon vanilla extract

Vegetable cooking spray

Preheat oven to 350°F. Spray an 8-inch square baking pan with vegetable cooking spray. Next, in a medium-sized bowl, combine the flour, cocoa, and salt. Mix well. Then, in a large bowl whisk together the eggs, sugar, applesauce, oil, and vanilla. Stir in the flour mixture from the medium bowl until the lumps are gone. Add the chocolate chips and stir until the chips are mixed into the batter. Once that's done, pour the batter in the 8-inch pan. Bake about 25 minutes or until a toothpick inserted into the center comes out clean. Carefully remove the pan from the oven and place it on a wire rack to cool for 20 minutes. Cut the brownies into squares and enjoy with a glass of milk! Ask your parents if they have any champagne glasses you may borrow. Serve the milk in champagne glasses for some extra-added glamour.

Sausage Cheese Muffins

Makes 12 muffins

3 tablespoons olive oil

2 sausage links, each sliced into six pieces

1 cup all-purpose flour

1 cup yellow cornmeal

1 cup grated Parmesan cheese

3 teaspoons baking powder

1 teaspoon salt

1 cup skim milk
1 large egg
2 egg whites

Preheat oven to 400°F. Spray a 12-cup muffin pan with vegetable cooking spray or line with paper liners. In a skillet, heat 1 tablespoon of oil and add the sausage links. Sauté until cooked through, about 7 minutes. Set cooked sausages aside to cool then cut each link into six pieces. In a medium bowl, combine flour, baking powder, and salt. In a large bowl, whisk together milk, 2 tablespoons of oil, egg and egg whites until smooth. Slowly add the flour mixture to the milk mixture, whisking just until a lumpy batter forms. Next, fill each muffin cup halfway with some batter. Place a piece of sausage in the center of each cup. Top the sausage piece with a bit of batter – enough to cover it. Bake muffins about 25 minutes or until the tops are golden and firm. Place pan on a wire rack and cool slightly. These muffins taste best when warm.

Party treats

Hand out mini telephone/address books.

SUPER SLEUTH PARTY

I was about 5 or 6 years old when I went to my first sleepover party. There was no theme. I was mostly excited to sleep over and wake up with my friends. I was mostly afraid of having nightmares.

Emily S.

The Puzzler

For each invitation you'll need an 8-inch by 11-inch piece of cardboard. Write out your invitation on each piece of cardboard:

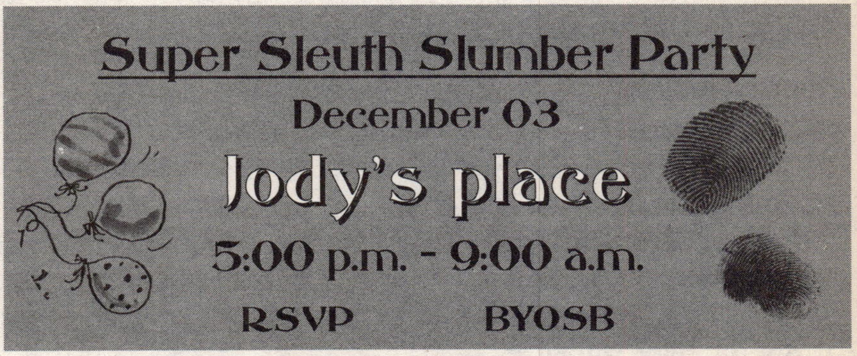

When you've finished writing out the invitations, cut each of them into different shapes and place the pieces in an envelope. Your friends will need to put the pieces of the puzzle together to figure out where and when the party is.

Who Did It?

Most toy and game stores sell Murder Mystery Games. If it's not too expensive, consider buying one and assigning roles to your friends as they arrive. If you don't want to buy a Murder Mystery Game then how about writing one of your own? The person to figure out who did it receives a prize, such as a mini puzzle.

Rent some video mysteries and watch them before going to bed.

Mystery Movies

Goonies
Ghostbusters
Harriet the Spy
Young Sherlock Holmes

I love sleepover parties! My friends and I talk about boys, put on fashion shows, and eat lots of junk food.

Jody K.

Secret Coded Treasure Hunt

Split your friends up into two teams and send them on a treasure hunt, but write down what they need to find in a secret code and have them decode the list! This will give the hunt an extra added challenge. Write down each letter of the alphabet in a column. Then, beside that column write the numbers 1– 26 beside your letter until you have filled up your column. This is the code key!

Code Key:

A 13	G 21	M 11	S 9	X 24
B 26	H 25	N 5	T 23	Y 15
C 18	I 20	O 2	U 8	Z 6
D 19	J 3	P 17	V 16	
E 14	K 12	Q 1	W 7	
F 22	L 4	R 10		

Dusting for Fingerprints

Did you know that no two people in the whole wide world have the same fingerprints?
Even identical twins. Teach your friends how to "lift" fingerprints. You'll need:

Clear adhesive tape

Black paper

Magnifying glass

First, find a fingerprint. The best place would be on a glass. Tear off a piece of clear tape big enough to cover the dusted print. Place the tape carefully over the print.

Gently lift up the tape – the print will lift up with it – and stick it onto the black paper.

Use your magnifying glass to examine the fingerprint. Notice all the different loops and whorls?

Recording Fingerprints

Send your friends home with a record of their fingerprints! You'll need:

Ink pad

Paper (for each person)

Each person's paper should be labeled for the right hand and left hand.

RIGHT HAND

Thumb Index Middle Ring Little

LEFT HAND

Thumb Index Middle Ring Little

Press each finger onto the ink pad and roll the finger from side to side. Next, press each finger firmly under the correct space. After you're all done compare fingerprints. Notice how different they look – even slightly!

Mysterious Mexican Menu

Snacks

Guacamole
Tortilla Chips

Dinner

Mystery Meat Enchiladas
Mixed Green Salad

Munchies

Nighttime Nachos

Breakfast

Fruity Fruit Shakes
Cinnamon Buns

Recipe Corner

Guacamole

Makes about 2½ cups

2 ripe avocados
Juice of 2 small limes
1 onion, finely chopped
2 small tomatoes, peeled, seeded, and chopped
Salt and pepper

Cut the avocados in half and twist to release from the seed. With a spoon, scoop out the pulp into a shallow bowl. Mash avocados with a fork. Add the lime juice, onions, and tomatoes. Mix well. Season with salt and pepper.

Mystery Meat Enchiladas

Serves 4 people (figure about 2 enchiladas per person)

4 medium tomatoes, seeded and chopped (about 2 cups)
2 medium red onions, chopped (about 2 cups)
1 medium red or green bell pepper, chopped (about 1 cup)
3 tablespoons red wine vinegar
1 pound lean ground beef or turkey
1 can (4 ounces) chopped green chillies, undrained
4 teaspoons chilli powder
1 can (15 ounces) crushed tomatoes
8 corn tortillas
1 cup shredded Monterey Jack cheese
Vegetable cooking spray

In a small bowl, combine fresh tomatoes, 1 cup of onion, bell pepper, and vinegar. Cover with some plastic wrap and let it stand for 30 minutes. Next, in a large nonstick skillet cook the meat over medium-high heat, stirring about 10 minutes or until no longer pink. Using a spoon, place beef or turkey on a plate. Preheat the oven to 400°F. Add the remaining onion (1 cup) to the skillet and sauté for about 3 minutes. Add chillies and chilli powder and stir for another 2 minutes. Now, add the beef or turkey and crushed tomatoes and simmer – stirring occasionally – for 15 minutes. Spray a large baking dish with vegetable cooking spray. Spoon the beef or turkey filling down the center of each tortilla. Once filled, rolled up the tortillas and place them seam down in the baking dish. You're now ready to use the fresh tomato mixture that has been standing for 30 minutes. Spoon it over the top of each tortilla and sprinkle with some cheese. Bake the tortillas for 10 minutes.

Nighttime Nachos

Serves 4

32 tortilla chips

1 cup shredded Monterey Jack cheese

1 cup shredded cheddar cheese

2 medium tomatoes, chopped

1 cup thinly sliced green onion

1 clove garlic, minced

2 tablespoons chopped fresh parsley or cilantro

1 tablespoon red wine vinegar

Preheat oven to 400°F. Place chips in a single layer on a nonstick baking sheet and set aside. In a small bowl, combine the Monterey Jack and cheddar cheeses. Set aside. In a medium bowl, combine the tomatoes, green onion, garlic, cilantro or parsley, and vinegar. Mix well. Place 2 teaspoons of salsa in the center of each chip and top each with some cheese. Bake chips in the oven until cheese has melted (about 4 minutes). Using a spatula, carefully place nachos on a serving platter. Olé!

Fruity Fruit Shakes

Serves 4 people

1 cup plain yogurt

1 cup skim milk

2 medium peaches or nectarines, sliced (about 2 cups)

1 cup fresh strawberries

1 banana, sliced

1 teaspoon vanilla extract

1 teaspoon ground cinnamon or nutmeg

4 ice cubes

In a blender, combine the yogurt, milk, peach or nectarine, strawberries, banana, vanilla extract, cinnamon or nutmeg, and ice cubes. Blend until smooth and foamy. If mixture is too thick add a few more ice cubes and blend a bit longer. Pour mixture into glasses and enjoy! Don't like peaches or strawberries? Well, use any fruit – just remember you need about 3 cups of fresh fruit in all.

Once you're all tucked safely into your sleeping bags – tell some ghost stories!

QUIZ: DO YOU ACT YOUR AGE?

Are you a baby or just a bit too mature for your own good?

1. Your mother has forbidden you to color your hair until you're 18! But when your

friend's sister – you know, the one who just graduated from beauty school – offers to do it for free, you

a. start begging and making promises about chores you'll do if she'll only say yes;

b. just go for it, without her permission. You're old enough to do as you please, and anyway what can she to you once it's done?

c. try to reason with her.

2. **You just bought the cutest sundress ever and think you look the bomb in it! That is until your older sister tries it on and even you can't stop looking at her! You**

a. don't tell her how great she looks – you just smile;

b. insist she take the dress off and vow never to lend her any of your clothes – ever!

c. tell her how lovely she looks and pray that in a couple of years you'll look like her.

3. You've had a crush on a boy who's in a grade below you. You just found out that, while he thinks you're really nice, he just wants to be friends – nothing more. You

a. admit your disappointment to your friends and make jokes about the girl that he does like;

b. refer to him as the "baby" from that point on;

c. realize it never could have worked and are happy with just being friends.

4. A major snowstorm hits your area and, woo-hoo, school is closed for the day. Your friends knock on your door carrying sleds and wearing the latest in fashion snowsuits. You

a. throw on your snow boots, run outside and begin throwing snowballs at them;

b. roll your eyes at your friends' childish idea to go

sledding. Today, you plan on catching up on your beauty sleep;

c. grab your sled and are out the door before you having a chance to tie your boots.

5. Your dad informs you that the family vacation to Hawaii has been postponed for at least two months – your mom's business partner has been called away on a family emergency and someone has to stay to run the company. You

a. say you understand, but decide to lay the guilt on your mom's business partner the next time you see her;

b. start screaming and crying and don't plan on ever stopping;

c. cry just a little bit – you don't want to make your mom feel any worse than she does already.

6. During a food fight in the school cafeteria some mystery meat lands right on your math book; you

a. wipe off your book and leave the cafeteria, but not before getting even with the kid who threw the meat at you in the first place;

b. start throwing your lunch in a fitful rage;

c. grab your stuff and head straight out of there – careful to dodge any more meat that may be flying through the air.

7. When people guess your age, they usually

a. get it right on the first try;

b. say you're younger than you are;

c. say you're older than you are.

8. As far as stuffed animals are concerned, you

a. think they look cute on the bed, but when it's time for you to go to sleep, they get the floor;

b. feel there are no words to describe just how much you love your fluffy-wuffies;

c. can't wait to sell them at your parent's next garage sale.

9. Your teacher humiliates you during class. At recess you

a. stick your tongue out behind her back and sheepishly smile the moment she turns around;

b. stick some chewed-up bubble gum on her seat and high five your friends when she runs to the teacher 's lounge to try to get it off;

c. complain about her to your best friend and try to put it behind you.

10. Your friends are supposed to leave you a message where to meet up with them once you're through baby-sitting for your next door neighbor. When you get home there's no message from them. You

a. are disappointed, but decide not to jump to any conclusions – you'll speak with them in the morning;

b. can't believe they didn't wait. You're not calling them for at least a week, and if they call you, they can talk to the dial tone;

c. don't really care 'cause they probably just went bowling and you're tired of all the immature boys they flirt with at the alley.

11. In your experience, the best way to get what you want from your parents is to

a. act all cute and charming and irresistible;

b. pout until they give in;

c. explain your feelings and if they don't give in you don't press the issue.

For each question you answered with the letter **(a)** give yourself **2** points

For each question you answered with the letter **(b)** give yourself **1** point

For each question you answered with the letter **(c)** give yourself **3** points.

Big Baby (11 to 21 points)

Screaming will not get you very far in life. You have yet to realize that some situations call for a certain amount of maturity.

Perfectly Primed (22 to 26 points)

You're aging gracefully. You radiate the perfect combination of cuteness and maturity. You take advantage of being young enough to have carefree fun without acting like a total child.

So Serious (27 to 31 points)

You're a wonderfully mature person, but remember, once you become an adult there's no turning back. Let loose and have some fun – you don't always have to do the mature thing!

COOL CRAFTS PARTY

I get afraid that I won't feel well in the middle of the night.

Erin S.

Since this is a crafts party let your imagination run wild when designing these invitations.

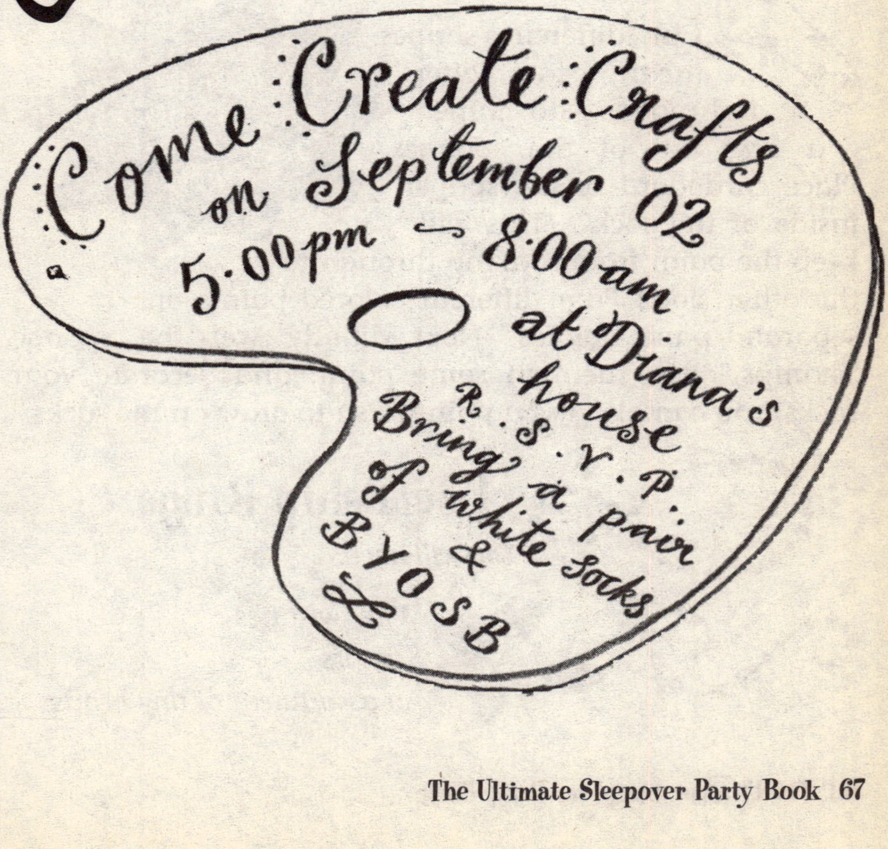

Sock Designs

You'll need:

Fabric paint
Sponges
Paper plates
Scissors
Paint brushes
Cardboard or newspaper

Cut different shapes (heart, star, letters, and moons – to name a few) out of the sponges. Place cardboard or newspaper inside of the socks. (This will keep the paint from soaking through to the other side.) Pour different colored paints on separate paper plates. Next, lightly wet the sponge "stamps," dab them in some paint, and decorate your socks. You can also use a paintbrush to draw on the socks.

Have some extra socks on hand in case any of your guests forget to bring their own.

Friendship Rings

You will need:

Wire twist ties
Scissors
An assortment of tiny beads

Peel all the plastic or paper off the wire twist ties. String beads onto the wire until it is long enough to wrap around a finger. Twist the ends together.

Draw names from a hat and exchange rings with the person you pick.

Tinted Glass

You'll need:

Tempera paints
White glue
Clear glass jar or glass cup
Paintbrushes
Clear liquid glaze (you can find this at an art supply store)

First, mix the paints with the glue – this will make the paints stick to the glass. You want to keep the paint thick so that it won't run. Next, paint any kind of design onto the glass. Once the paint has completely dried seal it by brushing on a coat of clear liquid glaze.

Bookmarks

You'll need:

Construction paper
Clear Con-Tact paper (optional)
Scissors
Ruler
Hole punch

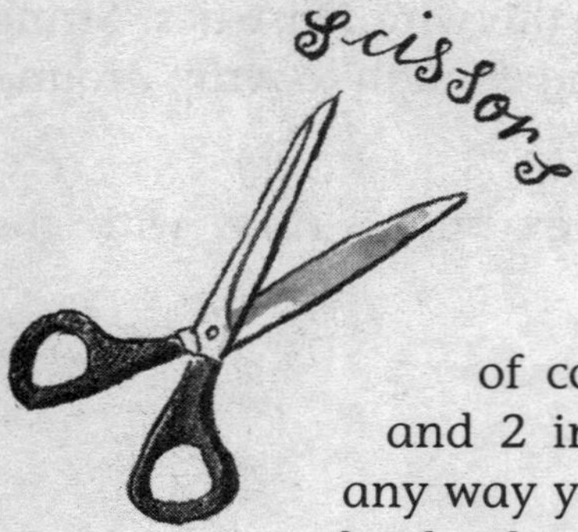

Ribbon
Stickers
Markers
Crayons

For each bookmark cut a piece of construction paper 6 inches long and 2 inches wide. Decorate both sides any way you like. For a glossy finish, cover the bookmark with clear Con-Tact paper. Punch a hole in the top and tie on a ribbon.

Homemade Finger Paints

You will need:

2 tablespoons sugar
1/3 cup cornstarch
2 cups cold water
1 cup clear dishwashing liquid
Food coloring

Mix the sugar and cornstarch together in a pan. Slowly, add the water. Stir it over low heat until the mixture becomes a smooth and clear gel – about 5 minutes. When the mixture is cool, stir in the dishwashing liquid. Scoop equal amounts into small cups and stir in the food coloring.

Set out lots of different colored paper, markers, paints, glue, beads, buttons, and crayons. Now, let your imaginations go wild!

All About Me and You

An *All About Me and You* book is a cool way for you and your friends to get to know everything about each other. Get an empty notebook and write down the following questions on the first page. Then, have everyone fill out the questions on their own sheets of paper in the book – once each person is finished filling out the *All About Me and You* book fold over her page so that no one can see her answers. When everyone is done, pass it around. Try to be as honest as possible.

Name:
Address:
Birthday:
School I Go To:
Favorite Subject:
Worst Subject:
Hobbies:
Sports I'm Good At:
Favorite Outfit:
Favorite Song:
Favorite Group:
Favorite Television Show:

Favorite Book:
Favorite Movie:
Favorite Actress:
Favorite Actor:
Best Friend:
Boy I Like:
Boy I Can't Stand:
In The Future I Plan On Being A:

Cool Crafts Cuisine

Snacks

Veggies and Dip
Yogurt-covered raisins
Granola

Munchies

Dinner

Pizza (order in or make your own)

Breakfast

Assorted Cereals
Recipe Corner

Pita Pizzas

You'll need:

(9–10 inch round) pita breads (one per person)
1 cup pizza or tomato sauce
2 cups shredded cheddar or mozzarella cheese
¾ cup chopped cooked vegetables (broccoli, zucchini, eggplant, and/or peppers)
1 cup chopped cooked meat (ham, turkey, chicken, salami, and/or sausage) (Vegetarians can skip the meat and just add more vegetables.)

Preheat the oven to 400° F. Split open each pita bread at its edges into two thin rounds. Arrange cut sides up on baking sheets. Spread each pita with 1 cup of sauce and sprinkle each with ½ cup of cheese. Top with a sprinkling of vegetables and meat. Bake five to eight minutes, until pizza is hot and the cheese is melted. Let it cool for 3 full minutes then serve.

Party Treats

You don't need them for this party. The cool crafts your friends make will be their treats.

ASTROLOGY PARTY

The sleepover party I remember most is the one where we waited until our friend who talked in her sleep fell asleep so we could ask her questions about boys.

-Carla A.

Handy Invitations

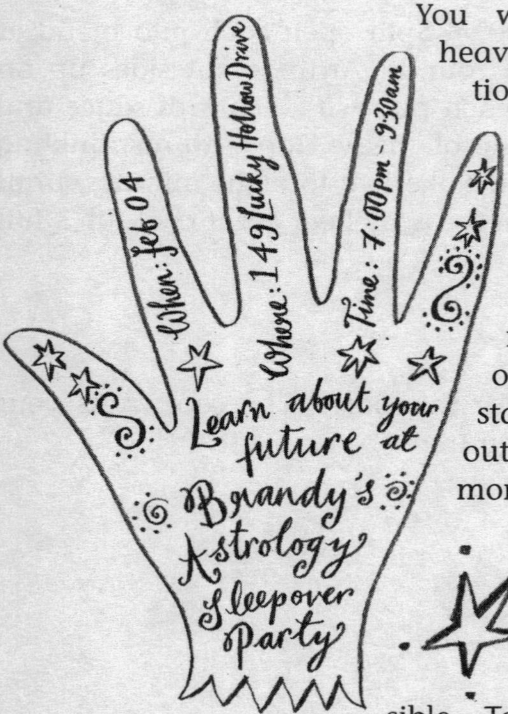

You will need a piece of heavy paper for each invitation. Trace your hand, cut it out, and write the invitation on the inside of the palm.

Decorate your party room with lots of paper moons, stars, and planets. Cut out that day's and month's horoscope from as many different magazines and newspapers (and look them up on the Internet) as possible. Tape them up on the wall. A couple of weeks before your party find out your friends' birthdays. Before your party, make a scroll out of white paper for each of your guests; include the figure for her sign along with her astrological traits.

Have your friends read them aloud and talk about whether her personality matches her sign. Or read aloud the traits from each sign and have everyone decide on who at your party fits that description. Are they right?

Aquarius (January 21 to February 19) (The Water Bearer)

Traits: friendly, humanitarian, honest, loyal, original, inventive, independent, intellectual, unpredictable, private, stubborn

Flower: orchid

Color: turquoise

Gemstone: aquamarine

Some Famous Aquarians:
Abraham Lincoln
Oprah Winfrey
Wolfgang Amadeus Mozart

Sagittarius (November 22 to December 21) (The Archer)

Traits: optimistic, independent, jovial and good-humored, honest, straightforward, philosophical, tactless, restless, irresponsible

Flower: dandelion

Color: purple

Gemstone: topaz

Some Famous Sagittarians:
Sir Winston Churchill
Brad Pitt
Britney Spears

Aries (March 21 to April 20) (The Ram)

Traits: adventurous, energetic, courageous, enthusiastic, confident, quick-witted, quick-tempered, impulsive, impatient, a daredevil

Flower: honeysuckle

Color: red

Gemstone: diamond

Some Famous Arians:
Charlie Chaplin
Marlon Brando
Thomas Jefferson

Leo (July 23 to August 22) (The Lion)

Traits: generous, warmhearted, creative, enthusiastic, faithful, loving, bossy, pompous, intolerant

Flower: sunflower

Color: gold

Gemstone: ruby

Some Famous Leos:
Napoleon Bonaparte
George Bernard Shaw
Mae West

Taurus (April 21 to May 21) (The Bull)

Traits: patient, reliable, warmhearted, loving, persistent, determined, jealous, possessive, inflexible, self-indulgent

Flower: pink rose

Color: pink

Gemstone: emerald

Some Famous Taureans:
Sigmund Freud
William Shakespeare
Malcolm X (Malik el Shabbaz)

Virgo (August 23 to September 23) (The Virgin)

Traits: modest, shy, meticulous, reliable, practical, creative, intelligent, perfectionist, conservative; a worrier

Flower: cornflower

Color: green and dark brown

Gemstone: sardonyx

Some Famous Virgoans:
Michael Jackson
D. H. Lawrence
Queen Elizabeth I

Capricorn (December 22 to January 20) (The Goat)

Traits: practical, ambitious, disciplined, patient, humorous, reserved, strong-willed, calm, pessimistic

Flower: pansy

Color: brown

Gemstone: black onyx

Some Famous Capricornians:
Louis Pasteur
Edgar Allan Poe
Elvis Presley

Gemini (May 22 to June 21) (The Twins)

Traits: adaptable, versatile, communicative, witty, intellectual, lively, nervous, inconsistent, inquisitive

Flower: lavender

Color: green

Gemstone: agate

Some Famous Geminians:
H.R.H. Philip, Duke of Edinburgh
Johnny Depp
Bob Dylan

Libra (September 24 to October 23) (The Scales)

Traits: romantic, charming, easygoing, sociable, idealistic, indecisive, gullible, flirtatious, self-indulgent

Flower: white rose

Color: blue

Gemstone: sapphire

Some Famous Librans:
Gwyneth Paltrow
Will Smith
Kate Winslet

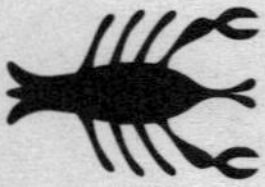

Cancer (June 22 to July 22) (The Crab)

Traits: emotional, loving, intuitive, imaginative, cautious, protective, sympathetic, moody, touchy, clingy

Flower: lily

Color: gray

Gemstone: pearl

Some Famous Cancerians:
Tom Cruise
Princess Diana
Nelson Mandela

Scorpio (October 24 to November 22) (The Scorpion)

Traits: determined, forceful, emotional, intuitive, powerful, exciting, jealous, compulsive, secretive

Flower: geranium

Color: dark red

Gemstone: opal

Some Famous Scorpios:
Marie Antoinette
Charles, Prince of Wales
Leonardo DiCaprio

Pisces (February 20 to March 20) (The Fishes)

Traits: imaginative, sensitive, compassionate, kind, selfless, sympathetic, idealistic, secretive, vague

Flower: moss

Color: sea green

Gemstone: moonstone

Some Famous Pisceans:
Elizabeth Taylor
Cindy Crawford
Kurt Cobain

Astrological Eats

Snacks

Fortune cookies
Beef (Taurus) Jerky
Sunflower seeds

Dinner

Fish (Pisces) and chips

Munchies

S'mores (marshmallows look like stars in the sky)
Angel Food Cake with whipped cream

Breakfast

Eggs (sunny side up)

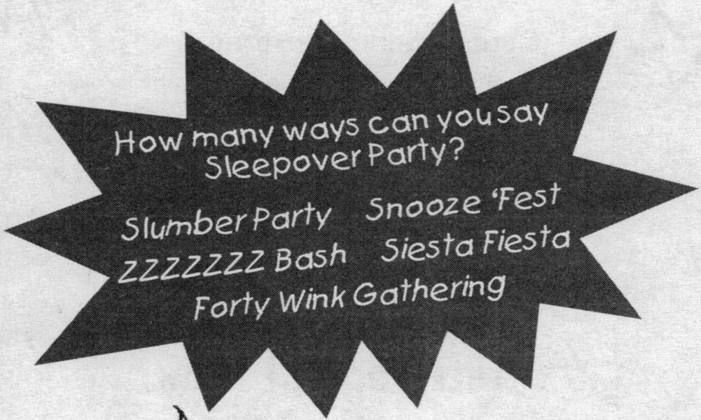

Palm Reading

Some say you can figure out your future just by looking at the lines on your palm. Just for fun, take turns telling the fortunes of your guests.

Life line: The little lines intersecting the main line on the palm are said to represent all different aspects of the

future. If the lifeline is long and deep, you will have a long and exciting life;
short and deep, you'll be very healthy;
far away from the thumb, you'll be popular;
straight and close to the thumb, you will have a protected life.

Love Line: The small lines that veer off from the main line. If the love line is long, you'll marry someone very rich;
short, you are very emotional;
strong and deep, you are very passionate.

Create a cozy corner in your party room filled with all your stuffed animals and with pillows from around the house. This will be a nice place for your friends to sit and chat.

Money Line: This line starts at the base of the thumb. If it runs to the index finger, you will be rich; runs to the middle finger, you'll be successful in business; runs to your little finger, you will inherit lots of money.

Time Capsule

What you'll need:

- a shoebox for each person
- paper, pens, pencils, crayons, markers, glue, ribbon

On a piece of paper everyone should write down the answers to the following questions.

1 Where do you live now?

2 Where do you think you'll be living in twenty years?

3 What is your favorite subject in school?

4 What do you think you'll be doing for a living when you are no longer in school?

5 What boy do you like?

6 Who is your favorite musical group?

7 What is your favorite song?

8 What was the best movie you ever saw?

9 What is your favorite television show?

10 Who is your best friend?

Have everyone place their answers in the shoebox, decorate it, and promise each other not to open it for the next twenty years.

Recipe Corner

S'mores

For about 15 S'mores you'll need:

1 jar marshmallow fluff

1 box graham crackers

1 bag mini chocolate bars

Gently spread some marshmallow fluff on a graham cracker. Place a chocolate bar on top of the marshmallow fluff and top with another graham cracker. A truly heavenly snack!

VALENTINE'S DAY PARTY

I hate having to get undressed in front of my friends.

Laurie P.

Valentine's Day Delights

Snack

Heart-shaped candies
Chocolate kisses
Sugar cookies

Dinner

Spaghetti with marinara sauce

Munchies

Strawberry ice cream sodas

Breakfast

Cinnamon buns

Have a Heart

Before your guests arrive cut many different colored pieces of paper into heart shapes. Hide them in different places throughout your party room. To play, each guest must collect as many pairs – two hearts of the same color – as she can. The person with the most pairs wins a prize.

What Would You Do If . . .?

Hand out index cards to all your friends and have each person write down a "what if . . ." question. Place all the index cards in a bowl and take turns drawing a card and answering the question. Some "what if . . ." questions:

What would you do if you found a wallet filled with one million dollars?

What would you do if you didn't like your best friend's boyfriend?

What would you do if you caught your brother stealing money out of your friend's backpack?

Macaroni Jewelry

Pull names from a hat and make a cool necklace or bracelet for the person whose name you picked.

Materials:

Uncooked macaroni
Tempera paint
Paint brushes
Kite string

Paint the macaroni with different colors and designs. Place each piece on a newspaper to dry. When they are dry string them on kite string to make bracelets and necklaces.

My first sleepover was on my 12th birthday, which is Valentine's Day. It was a red and heart theme party. We pulled names from a hat and made friendship bracelets for each other.

Lisa R.

Recipe Corner

Strawberry Ice Cream Sodas

For each soda you will need:

1 cup milk
1 cup sparkling water
2 scoops strawberry ice cream

Mix the milk and water together, and add the ice cream.

Sugar Cookies

1 cup butter
1 cup white sugar
1 cup brown sugar
1 egg
1 teaspoon baking powder
1 teaspoon vanilla
3 cups flour
1 teaspoon salt

In a large bowl mix all of the ingredients together. Then roll mixture into 1-inch balls. On a greased cookie tray space the balls about 2 inches apart. Next, press each cookie with a fork. Bake at 350°F for 12 minutes or until the edges turn brown. Watch carefully so that the cookies don't burn. Take out of the oven and let cool.

VALENTINE QUIZ:

IS HE THE BOY FOR YOU?

1. **You just missed school for a whole week due to the worst cold ever. The boy you like is in your history class. When you ask to borrow his notes, he**
   a. agrees and reminds you not to lose them;
   b. hands them to you with a smile and says that he noticed you were out;
   c. points to his desk and says, "they're right over there."

2. **Your best friend is throwing the party of the millennium. You gather all of your courage and personally hand the boy you like an invitation. He says**

a. "looks like a cool party – let me see what my buddies are doing that evening;"
b. "wouldn't miss it!"
c. "will there be any other cute girls besides you at this thing?"

3. It's Saturday night and you're out with your grandparents. Across the street is the boy you like and when you finally catch his eye, he
a. waves hello;
b. does a funny dance that he knows will just crack you up;
c. nods his head. But, who could blame him – you are with your grandparents.

4. A group of you is going to the movies and by some stroke of luck, and sly maneuvering, you and the boy you like are sitting right next to each other!
During the movie he
a. he looks over at you a few times and nervously smiles;

b. playfully grabs your fingers whenever you take more popcorn from the bucket he's holding;
c. doesn't say one word – he's deeply involved in the story line.

5. At the annual school dance, the boy you like

a. shyly asks you to dance;
b. won't let anyone but him dance with you;
c. cuts in between all your other partners.

6. At the community swimming pool you start to panic in the deep end. The guy you like

a. yells for the lifeguard's attention;
b. jumps in after you;
c. extends his leg and pulls you in.

7. A group of you and your friends are out shopping at the mall. When you go up to the register to pay for the CD you've been dying to own, you realize you're a bit short on cash. The guy you like

a. hands you some money and says, "take your time paying me back;"
b. hands you some money and says, "don't you even dare think of paying me back;"
c. opens up his wallet, shows you it's empty, and sheepishly smiles.

8. **When the guy you like finds out you're throwing the ultimate sleepover party that night for your girlfriends, he**
   a. tells you to have a great time;
   b. asks if he could come too;
   c. drops over with some of his friends.

9. **Uh-oh! Pop quiz in math. When your teacher isn't looking you glance over at the boy you like's exam. He**
   a. lets you copy, but gives you a disappointing nod;
   b. carefully shows you the answers
   c. lets you copy and you end up passing, but barely.

0. **You and the boy you like are finally out on a date. Afterward, you realize**
   a. he's nice, but not as fun as when he's with a group;
   b. this could be the love of your life;
   c. he's a lot of fun, but you barely got a word in the whole afternoon.

Scoring

For every question you answered with the letter (a) give yourself 2 points.

For every question you answered with the letter (b) give yourself 3 points.

For every question you answered with the letter (c) give yourself 1 point.

THIS BOY IS A KEEPER
30 – 21 points

This boy has lots of personality, is an individual and it's obvious that he likes you a lot! Have fun, take it slow, and be yourself.

THERE'S HOPE 20 – 11 points

The boy you like isn't that secure when it comes to girls, but he does get some points for trying. It seems as if he likes you, but he has a difficult time showing his true feelings or maybe he's just confused. Give him some time – he may surprise you.

RUN AS FAST AS YOU CAN
10 points and under

This guy is not for you! In fact, he's not for anybody! Who wants someone who is only interested in himself and impressing his friends with being cool and rude? Girlfriend, find yourself another boy!

PICNIC PARTY

Junk food is the key to a great sleepover party!

Helene B.

If the weather is good consider sleeping outside after your picnic. Don't panic if it rains – indoor picnics are just as much fun as outdoor ones. Just spread some blankets and listen to the raindrops.

Picnic Party Invitations

For each invitation you will need an 8-inch by 11-inch piece of paper. Draw a gingham border or one with ladybugs. Roll up the invitations and tie them up with some twine.

Picnic Party Menu

Snack

Mini hotdogs with a side of mustard for dipping (Can't find mini hotdogs? Just cut a hotdog in thirds.)

Dinner

Honey Chicken Wings
Potato Salad
Corn on the Cob

Munchies

Trail Mix

Breakfast

Cinnamon French Toast

As much as I love sleepover parties I get real homesick sleeping away from my house. I feel kind of stupid saying that — especially since I'm almost 12 years old. I usually get a funny feeling inside of me when my friends and I are getting ready for bed. I begin to wonder what my mom and dad are doing back home and if they miss me. I just try and snuggle up with my pillow and think about what a good time I'm having with all of my friends.

Lace B.

Shell Painting

Painting shells is a fun project to make with your friends or you can make them beforehand and use as weights during the picnic to keep napkins from blowing away with the wind.

You'll need:

Seashells

Acrylic paints

Paintbrushes

Before you begin make sure the seashells are clean and dry. Paint pictures on the inside of each shell. Let them dry.

While your friends are eating breakfast hide a special note of thanks in their overnight bag

Treasure Hunt

Before your guests arrive hide around your party area the following treasures: leaves, twigs, pinecones, dried flowers, and shells. Tie a note with ribbon to each treasure giving a clue to where the next one might be. Once all the items have been found use them to decorate small terra cotta pots which can be found at your local garden nursery. These will make nice party treats for your guests.

Bug Bites

As your friends arrive hand them a sheet of colored dot stickers (20 dots per person will be just perfect). The object of the game is to get rid of all your dots. When someone isn't

looking stick a dot on her, but don't get caught because then she'll have to give you a dot bite. The first person to get rid of all her dots wins a prize.

Ha, Ha, Ha

Sit in a circle. One player begins by saying, "Ha"; the person to the right continues with, "Ha, Ha"; the next follows with, "Ha, Ha, Ha," and so on around the circle with each person adding another "Ha". Each player must pronounce the "Ha" as seriously as possible to avoid laughing as long as possible. Any player who laughs or makes any mistake must drop out of the "Ha Ha" circle. However, now she gets to try in any way, except for touching, to make the players still in the circle laugh. The last person left in the circle is the winner.

Recipe Corner

Honey Chicken Wings

You'll need:

8 chicken wings (figure about 4 wings per person)
½ cup honey sauce

Rinse chicken wings and pat them dry. Place them in a single layer on a baking pan. Brush the tops with honey sauce and bake at 375°F in a pre-heated oven for 20 minutes. Have an adult turn the wings and brush again with honey sauce. Bake for an additional 15 minutes, or until chicken is tender.

Honey Sauce

You'll need:

6 tablespoons catsup
1 tablespoon honey
1 tablespoon vinegar
1 pinch garlic salt

Stir all ingredients together and brush on chicken before cooking.

Trail Mix

You'll need:

1 cup granola
1 cup chocolate or carob chips
2 cups dried fruit
1 cup assorted nuts

Mix all of the ingredients together and enjoy!

TALENT SHOW PARTY

I get most excited about sleeping in my sleeping bag and seeing my friend's older brothers in the morning.

Melanie H.

This is a great way for you and your friends to show off your very special talents. Once your friends RSVP, find out what they will be doing as their talent. This will allow you to "introduce" them the night of the party.

Setting the Stage . . . Literally

Look around your house or backyard to see where you will be able to have an area serve as a "stage" and where you will be able to have room for your friends to sit in the "audience."

Tape each talent act and watch it before going to bed

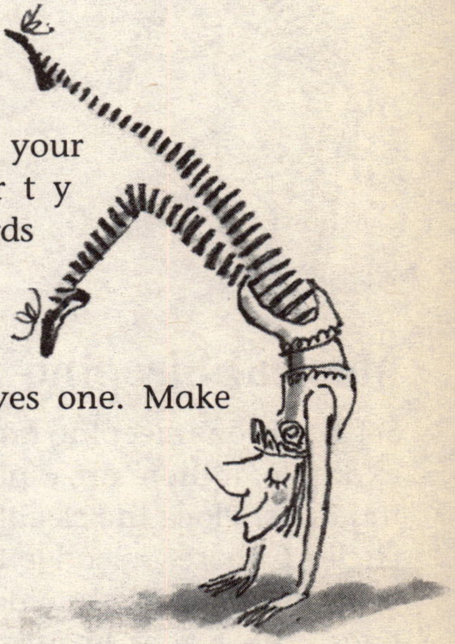

Before your party have awards made to be handed out to each person. Make sure to make enough awards so that everybody receives one. Make awards for:

Wackiest Talent
Most Talented
Cutest Costume
Most Original Performance

Tasty Talent Show Treats

Snack

Cookies
Corn Chips with Salsa

Dinner

Macaroni and Cheese
Green Salad

Munchies

Hot Pretzels

Breakfast

Scrambled Eggs
Hash Browns

Musical Sleeping Bags

Set down one sleeping bag for every player except one. For example, if there are 6 players then only set out five sleeping bags. Place the sleeping bags in a straight line or in a circle. Choose a leader to play the music. Before beginning, the players should be standing around the sleeping bags. The leader begins the music and the players walk around the sleeping bags in one direction. After a moment, the leader surprises the players by turning the music off. This is a signal to the players to find a sleeping bag as quickly as possible and to lie down! The player left without a sleeping bag is eliminated from the game. One sleeping bag is then removed in order to keep the number of sleeping bags one less than that of the players. A player and a sleeping bag is removed with each round until two players are left with the last sleeping bag. The player to lie down in this last sleeping bag is the winner.

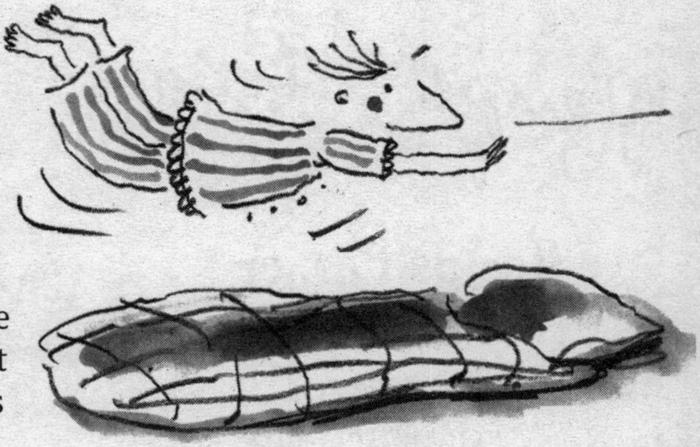

Acting Out

Play some of your favorite CDs and lip-sync along with the band. Go wild!

Casting Director

Pretend you and your friends are casting directors and Hollywood is planning to make movies out of your favorite books. Who would you cast? Write it down on pieces of paper and see whether you and your friends chose the same stars.

Sometimes when we play hide and go seek we spit water in the face of whoever finds us.

Madeline G.

Recipe Corner

Recipe Corner

Hot Pretzels

You'll need:

1 cup warm water
2 packages active dry yeast
2 tablespoons sugar
3 cups all-purpose flour
2 cups butter or shortening
1 egg
Coarse salt (kosher salt)

Pour the cup of very warm water into a large mixing bowl and add the yeast. Stir until the yeast is completely dissolved. Add the sugar and stir. Gradually add the flour and stir. As you are adding the last of the flour, the dough will become stiff and dry – that's how you want it to be. Sprinkle some flour on the counter top or on a breadboard and flour your hands. Now knead the dough for about five minutes by pressing it flat with the heels of your hands, folding the flattened dough in half, and then pressing it flat again. Form the dough into a ball, put it back into the bowl, cover the bowl with a dishtowel, and place the bowl in a warm, dark place for at least thirty minutes. The rising dough will almost double in size. While the dough is rising, preheat the oven to 400°F. Grease or butter a cookie sheet. When the dough has risen, put it back on the floured breadboard or counter. Flour a rolling pin and roll out the dough into an approximate square about one-fourth to one-half inch thick. Using the dull back of a table knife, cut the dough with a back and forth sawing motion into strips about as wide as your fattest fingers. Your don't have to be exact. Twist each shape into a pretzel shape and pinch the ends together. As you handle the long strips of dough, try not to let them stretch too thin. Place the pretzel-shaped dough on the greased cookie sheet. Beat the egg in a small bowl for a minute, and with a pastry brush coat the top of each pretzel with the egg. Now sprinkle the salt, to your liking, over the pretzels. Bake the pretzels for about twelve to fifteen minutes or until they are golden brown. Wait for them to cool off a bit before eating.

I love playing board games all night long.

Erica G.

BEAUTY QUIZ: DO YOU KNOW WHAT'S BEST FOR THE OUTER YOU?

1. What should you use to cleanse your skin?

a. the strongest cleanser available
b. a mild soap
c. exfoliating facial scrub
d. plain tap water.

2. How often should you change your skin-care program?

a. at least twice a year
b. when you have breakouts
c. on a daily basis
d. never. If it works now, why change it?

3. What kind of soap should you use to kill germs and bacteria on your hands?

a. antibacterial soap

b. moisturizing soap

c. soap shaped like seashells

d. any of the above.

4. What functions should a lip balm perform?

a. Create a moisture barrier;

b. Alleviate tingling and itching caused by chapped lips;

c. Act as an antiseptic;

d. All of the above.

5. Which of the following statements about sunscreens is true?

a. It doesn't matter how much sunscreen you use, as long as you use some;

b. You should use a lower sun protection factor (SPF) if you have darker skin;

c. A combination moisturizer/sunscreen is as good as two separate products;

d. If your skin stings after you apply sunscreen, that means it's working.

6. Which of the following is a quick, inexpensive fix for dry, brittle nails?

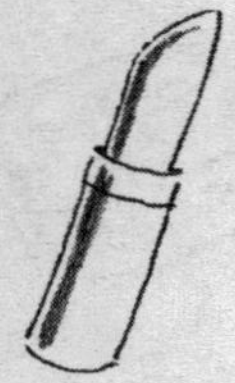

a. Scrub them with a soft-bristled toothbrush;

b. Apply petroleum jelly to them;

c. Sleep with gloves on;

d. Soak them in water.

7. What is the best way to file your nails?

a. Using back-and-forth strokes;

b. Applying hard strokes after soaking your hands in warm water;

c. Beginning on the sides and brushing towards the center, using light strokes in the same direction;

d. It's best not to file at all.

Beauty Quiz Answer Key

1. (b) A mild soap

2. (a) At least twice a year

3. (d) Any of the above

4. (d) All of the above

5. (c) A combination moisturize/sunscreen is as good as two separate products.

6. (b) Apply petroleum jelly to them

7. (c) Beginning on the sides and brushing toward the center, using light strokes in the same direction

NEW YEAR'S EVE PARTY

I love having sleepover parties at my house. My older sister scares my friends and me big time!

Cali A.

It's time to ring in the New Year and who better to celebrate with than your gal pals!

New Year's eve is a time of reflection of the year that has just passed and a celebration of the coming of change and good times.

Make a sit down dinner and talk about what you liked best and least about this past year. Discuss what you hope and think will happen in your lives and around the world in the New Year. Serve sparkling grape juice in wineglasses and take turns making a toast.

New Year's Resolutions

What's a resolution? Well, it's sort of like a promise, but not really. It's one thing or many things you decide or resolve or promise to do in the coming new year. Hand out some paper and have everyone write down three New Year's resolutions – then place all the resolutions in a hat. One person reads the resolutions aloud and have everyone guess whose resolution it is. The person who guesses the most correctly wins a prize.

My New Year's Resolutions are to:

1) hand all my homework in on time
2) be nicer to my sister
3) make a new friend

New Year's Eve Dinner

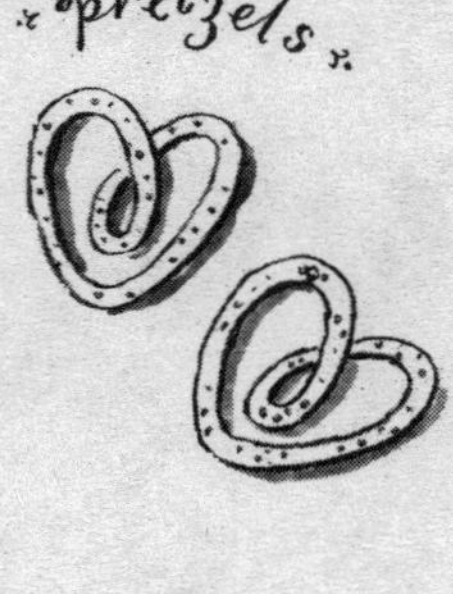

Appetizers

French Bread Pizzas

Dinner

Caesar Salad
Chicken Parmigiana

New Year Munchies

Chocolate Cupcakes

Breakfast

Bagels and Cream Cheese

Since New Year's Eve is a time of celebration, then grab your dancing shoes and put on the music. Dance the night away. Organize a dance contest – give a prize to the best dancer.

Hand out disposable cameras as your friends arrive so they can have their own New Year memories to take home with them.

New Year's Shakers

You'll need:

Dried beans, buttons, and brightly colored beads
2 clear plastic drinking cups (per noisemaker)
Colored Tape

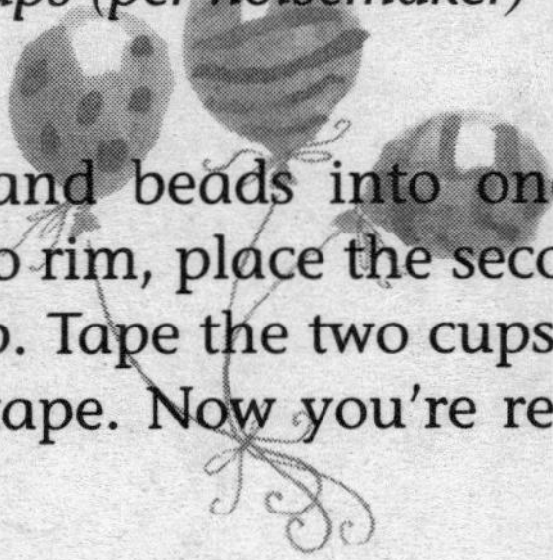

Pour beans, buttons, and beads into one of the plastic cups. Matching it rim to rim, place the second clear cup on top of the first clear cup. Tape the two cups tightly together with strips of colorful tape. Now you're ready to shake in the New Year!

Recipe Corner

French Bread Pizzas

Serves 4
You'll need:

1 loaf French or Italian bread

2 cups shredded mozzarella cheese

1 teaspoon dried oregano

1 8-ounce can of tomato sauce

In a saucepan warm up the tomato sauce over low heat. Preheat the oven to 350°F. Slice bread loaf in half horizontally, then in half-crosswise to form 4 slices. Place the bread on a baking sheet. Spread sauce evenly over bread slices; sprinkle with cheese and oregano. Bake in the oven until the cheese melts – about 10 minutes. Serve immediately.

Party Treats

This is an easy one – a new calendar!

PARTY DO'S AND DON'TS

Hostess Dos

- Make all your guests feel welcome;
- Show your friends where the bathroom is – use a nightlight;
- Be prepared with lots of games, activities, and videos;
- Make sure you have extra batteries around for your CD player.

3:00 a.m. was the latest I ever stayed up! I was so tired when my mom picked me up.

-Nicholette K.

Hostess Don'ts

- Don't be cliquey;
- Don't starve your guests – double check with your friends in case they have any food allergies;
- Don't torture your baby brother with super scary ghost stories – unless he's a real pain in the neck;
- Don't make anybody feel stupid about being homesick.

Besides the parties suggested in this book there are so many other kinds you can give. Feel free to take some ideas from one party and apply it to another. Now, it's *your* turn to plan the menu, invitations, decorations, and games. Here are just a few party theme ideas:

Hawaiian Luau

Let's Rock! Dance Party

Cooking Party

Birthday Party

Princess/Tea Party

Island Party

Dinner Party

Magic Night Party

Christmas and Hanukah Party

Halloween/Costume Party

Easter Egg Hunt Party

Summer's Over Party

Wild West Party

Sports Party

Flashlight Fun

All you need are batteries and some imagination.

- Wiggle your hands and see who can make the silliest shape on the wall.
- Make up signals to flash in the dark. For example, four long flashes mean, "I gotta go to the bathroom."

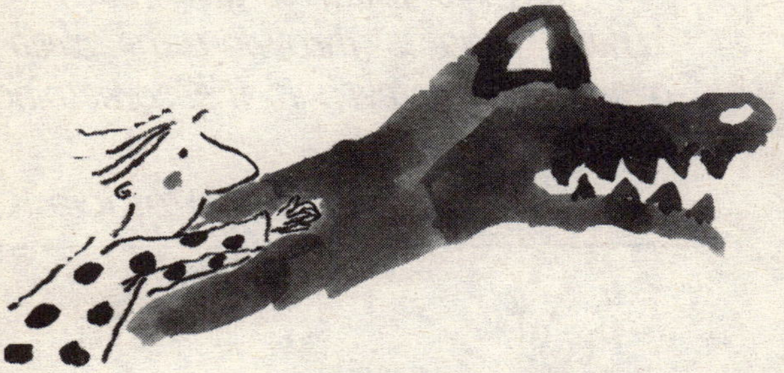

- Set the flashlights up like spotlights and take turns singing and dancing.
- Flashlight limbo

Party Pranks

Party pranks are not intended to be done in meanness – just in the spirit of good fun. Don't do any pranks on your friends if they are sensitive and won't appreciate it in the spirit they are intended.

- *Truth or Dare*: sit around in a circle and take turns choosing either truth or dare.

- *Dip the hand, of the first person to fall asleep, in warm water*: this will make her wake up and have to go to the bathroom.
- *Sleep Talkers:* do any of your friends talk in their sleep? Wait till they fall asleep and then start asking questions.

- *Shaving Cream:* put some shaving cream in your friend's palm once she's fallen asleep . . . let's not hope she has an itch in the middle of the night!

Always bring a gift for your friend who is throwing the sleep-over party — even if it's something small.

Patricia K.

PARTY MEMORIES

- You may have a great memory now, but just to be on the safe side there are many cool ways to remember your party.
- Buy an inexpensive white pillowcase and some fabric markers. As your friends arrive have them sign their name. Don't forget to put the date and anything else you want to remember about the party on the pillowcase.

- As your friends arrive, have your mom or dad take two Polaroid pictures of you with each of your guests. Keep one for yourself and give one to your friend as a party favor.

- Get a big piece of cardboard and have everyone sign in as they arrive.
- Videotape the party.

- Take lots of photos and put them in an album. Write funny captions beneath some of the photos.

- Hang a large sheet of paper on the wall with some masking tape, and place stickers, markers, and crayons near by. By the next morning you'll have a cool party souvenir.

Truth or Dare is really fun to play. I always pick the dares and my best friend always picks the truths.

Lori K.

The following pages give some ideas of how you and your guests can make records of the party you've had. Maybe you can think of other things to mention as well.

MY SLEEPOVER PARTY

My Name: ....

My Address: ....

Party Theme: ....

Date of Party: ....

Food I Served: ....

Friends I Invited: ....

Friends Who Came: ....

My Best Friend Is: ....

Games We Played: ....

.... **Fell Asleep First**

.... **Fell Asleep Last**

Funniest Moment: ....

Scariest Moment: ....

CDs We Listened To: ....

Pajamas I Wore: ....

Party Treats: ....

Stuff We Talked About:..

Boys We Talked About:..

....Wore The Cutest Pajamas

They Looked Like: ....

Gifts I Received: ....

Best Thing About My Party: ....

At the end of your party, have your guests fill out your sleepover sign-in book.

MY SLEEPOVER SIGN-IN

Name: ....

Address: ....

Favorite Food I Ate: ....

Favorite Game I Played: ....

My Best Friend Is: ....

Funniest Moment: ....

Scariest Moment: ....

The Pajamas I Wore: ....

My Sleepover Sign-In

Name: ....

Address: ....

Favorite Food I Ate: ....

Favorite Game I Played: ....

My Best Friend Is: ....

Funniest Moment: ....

Scariest Moment: ....

The Pajamas I Wore: ....

My Sleepover Sign-In

Name: ....

Address: ....

Favorite Food I Ate: ....

Favorite Game I Played: ....

My Best Friend Is: ....

Funniest Moment: ....

Scariest Moment: ....

The Pajamas I Wore: ....

My Sleepover Sign-In

Name: ....

Address: ....

Favorite Food I Ate: ....

Favorite Game I Played: ....

My Best-Friend Is: ....

Funniest Moment: ....

Scariest Moment: ....

The Pajamas I Wore: ....